The Sky

by Lisa Oram

PEARSON
Scott
Foresman

The Day Sky

Look up at the sky. What does it look like now?

The day sky and night sky are different. The sky is bright in the day. The **Sun** is a big ball of hot gas. It makes the day sky bright.

Sometimes you can see the Moon in the day sky. Most of the time you can see the Moon at night.

The Sun

The Sun is bigger than Earth. The Sun looks small to us. It is far away.

Earth gets light from the Sun. Earth gets heat from the Sun too.

The Sun seems to move in the sky. This is because Earth is moving. Where is the Sun in the sky over you now?

Day and Night

Earth turns around and around. This is called **rotation.**

One rotation takes Earth one day. We do not feel Earth moving. But it turns very fast!

Earth rotates. There is day and night. Part of Earth faces the Sun. Part of Earth faces away from the Sun. It is day for one part. It is night for the other part.

The flashlight is like the Sun. The globe is like Earth. The light shines on one side. When the globe turns, the other side gets the light. The side in the light has day.

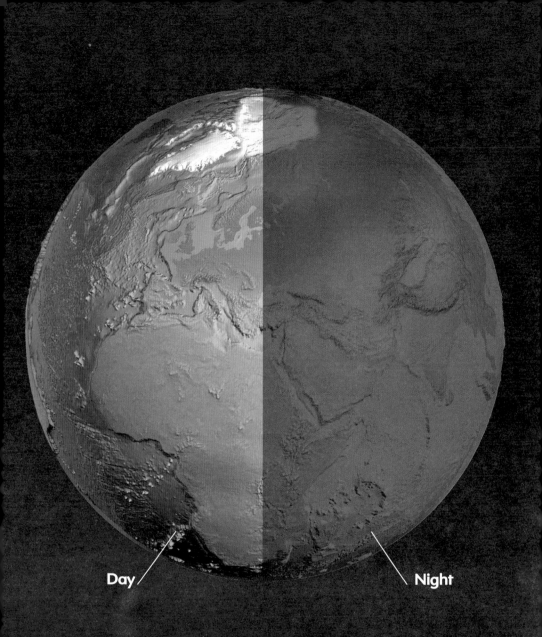

Day

Night

It is always day for half of Earth. It is always night for the other half of Earth. Day and night happen because Earth turns.

The Night Sky

Sometimes, we can see stars in the night sky. We can see planets too.

This cloud of gas is called a nebula.

A star is a ball of hot gas. Stars give off light. The Sun is a star. The Sun is the closest star to Earth.

Some people make wishes when they see stars!

Mercury

Venus

Earth

Ma

Earth is a planet. Earth moves around the Sun. Seven other planets do too. Planets do not give off light.

Jupiter

Uranus

Neptune

Saturn

Some planets are hard to see from Earth. **Telescopes** help people see things from far away. Telescopes make things in the sky look closer to Earth.

The Moon

The Moon is far away. But we do not need a telescope to see it. The Moon moves around Earth.

The Moon is not a planet. The Moon is not a star. The Moon has no air, plants, or animals.

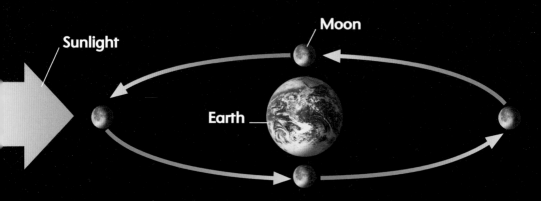

Sunlight

Moon

Earth

The Moon moves around Earth.

Humans have walked on the Moon.

The Sun lights part of the Moon. This is the part we see. The Moon looks different each night. It looks round and full. Then it looks thin. Then it looks full again. The Moon is full again every twenty-nine days or so.

Look up. What can you see in the sky now?

Glossary

Moon   a round object in the sky that moves around Earth

planet   an object in the sky that moves around the Sun

rotation   turning around and around

star   a big ball of hot gas

Sun   a big hot ball of gas that makes the day sky bright

telescope   a tool to use to make things that are far away look closer